C000121728

A CENTURY *of*
SWANSEA

University students on their way to stage a sit-in at Swansea University in February 1979. The University had avoided the student protests of ten years earlier, but these students were calling for more say in running the campus. (*Western Mail and Echo*)

A CENTURY *of* SWANSEA

JOHN O'SULLIVAN

SUTTON PUBLISHING

First published in the United Kingdom in 2000 by Sutton Publishing Limited

This new paperback edition first published in 2007 by
Sutton Publishing, an imprint of NPI Media Group
Cirencester Road · Chalford · Stroud · Gloucestershire · GL6 8PE

Copyright © John O'Sullivan, 2000, 2007
Copyright © 'Britain: A Century of Change', Roger Hudson, 2000, 2007

All rights reserved. No part of this publication may be reproduced, stored in a retrieval system, or transmitted, in any form or by any means, electronic, mechanical, photocopying, recording or otherwise, without the prior permission of the publisher and copyright holder.

The author has asserted the moral right to be identified as the author of this work.

British Library Cataloguing in Publication Data
A catalogue record for this book is available from the British Library.

ISBN 978-07509-4923-1

Front endpaper: Mumbles Head in the 1920s. (*Western Mail and Echo*)
Back endpaper: Aerial view of Swansea showing the Guildhall, *c.* 1959. (*Western Mail and Echo*)
Half title page: This statue of Captain Cat, the blind old sea dog from Dylan Thomas's *Under Milk Wood*, can be seen at Swansea Marina. (*Western Mail and Echo*)
Title page: Dylan Thomas statue, outside the theatre that bears his name. (*Western Mail and Echo*)

*This book is dedicated
to my late parents,
May and Din O'Sullivan*

The sundial in Singleton Educational Gardens in 1959. (*Western Mail and Echo*)

Typeset in Photina.
Typesetting and origination by
Sutton Publishing.
Printed and bound in England.

Contents

Firemen tackling a blaze after the third night's attack on the city by German bombers, 21 February 1941. The censors would not allow this picture to be published at the time. (*Western Mail and Echo*)

Britain: A Century of Change

Two women encumbered with gas masks go about their daily tasks during the early days of the war. (*Hulton Getty Picture Collection*)

The sixty years ending in 1900 were a period of huge trans-
formation for Britain. Railway stations, post-and-telegraph offices,
police and fire stations, gasworks and gasometers, new livestock
markets and covered markets, schools, churches, football grounds,
hospitals and asylums, water pumping stations and sewerage plants
totally altered the urban scene, and the country's population tripled with
more than seven out of ten people being born in or moving to the towns.
The century that followed, leading up to the Millennium's end in 2000,
was to be a period of even greater change.

When Queen Victoria died in 1901, she was measured for her coffin
by her grandson Kaiser Wilhelm, the London prostitutes put on black
mourning and the blinds came down in the villas and terraces spreading
out from the old town centres. These centres were reachable by train
and tram, by the new bicycles and still newer motor cars, were connected by the new telephone, and lit by gas or even electricity. The
shops may have been full of British-made cotton and woollen clothing
but the grocers and butchers were selling cheap Danish bacon,
Argentinian beef, Australasian mutton and tinned or dried fish and fruit
from Canada, California and South Africa. Most of these goods were
carried in British-built-and-crewed ships burning Welsh steam coal.

As the first decade moved on, the Open Spaces Act meant more parks,
bowling greens and cricket pitches. The First World War transformed
the place of women, as they took over many men's jobs. Its other
legacies were the war memorials which joined the statues of Victorian
worthies in main squares round the land. After 1918 death duties and
higher taxation bit hard, and a quarter of England changed hands in
the space of only a few years.

The multiple shop – the chain store – appeared in the high street:
Sainsburys, Maypole, Lipton's, Home & Colonial, the Fifty Shilling Tailor,
Burton, Boots, W.H. Smith. The shopper was spoilt for choice, attracted
by the brash fascias and advertising hoardings for national brands like
Bovril, Pears Soap, and Ovaltine. Many new buildings began to be seen,
such as garages, motor showrooms, picture palaces (cinemas), 'palais de
dance', and ribbons of 'semis' stretched along the roads and new
bypasses and onto the new estates nudging the green belts.

During the 1920s cars became more reliable and sophisticated as well
as commonplace, with developments like the electric self-starter making
them easier for women to drive. Who wanted to turn a crank handle in
the new short skirt? This was, indeed, the electric age as much as the
motor era. Trolley buses, electric trams and trains extended mass
transport and electric light replaced gas in the street and the home,
which itself was groomed by the vacuum cleaner.

A major jolt to the march onward and upward was administered by
the Great Depression of the early 1930s. The older British industries –

textiles, shipbuilding, iron, steel, coal – were already under pressure from foreign competition when this worldwide slump arrived. Luckily there were new diversions to alleviate the misery. The 'talkies' arrived in the cinemas; more and more radios and gramophones were to be found in people's homes; there were new women's magazines, with fashion, cookery tips and problem pages; football pools; the flying feats of women pilots like Amy Johnson; the Loch Ness Monster; cheap chocolate and the drama of Edward VIII's abdication.

Things were looking up again by 1936 and new light industry was booming in the Home Counties as factories struggled to keep up with the demand for radios, radiograms, cars and electronic goods, including the first television sets. The threat from Hitler's Germany meant rearmament, particularly of the airforce, which stimulated aircraft and aero engine firms. If you were lucky and lived in the south, there was good money to be earned. A semi-detached house cost £450, a Morris Cowley £150. People may have smoked like chimneys but life expectancy, since 1918, was up by 15 years while the birth rate had almost halved.

In some ways it is the little memories that seem to linger longest from the Second World War: the kerbs painted white to show up in the

A W.H.Smith shop front in Beaconsfield, 1922.

blackout, the rattle of ack-ack shrapnel on roof tiles, sparrows killed by bomb blast. The biggest damage, apart from London, was in the south-west (Plymouth, Bristol) and the Midlands (Coventry, Birmingham). Postwar reconstruction was rooted in the Beveridge Report which set out the expectations for the Welfare State. This, together with the nationalisation of the Bank of England, coal, gas, electricity and the railways, formed the programme of the Labour government in 1945.

Times were hard in the late 1940s, with rationing even more stringent than during the war. Yet this was, as has been said, 'an innocent and well-behaved era'. The first let-up came in 1951 with the Festival of Britain and there was another fillip in 1953 from the Coronation, which incidentally gave a huge boost to the spread of TV. By 1954 leisure motoring had been resumed but the Comet – Britain's best hope for taking on the American aviation industry – suffered a series of mysterious crashes. The Suez debacle of 1956 was followed by an acceleration in the withdrawal from Empire, which had begun in 1947 with the Independence of India. Consumerism was truly born with the advent of commercial TV and most homes soon boasted washing machines, fridges, electric irons and fires.

The *Lady Chatterley* obscenity trial in 1960 was something of a straw in the wind for what was to follow in that decade. A collective loss of inhibition seemed to sweep the land, as the Beatles and the Rolling Stones transformed popular music, and retailing, cinema and the theatre were revolutionised. Designers, hair-dressers, photographers and models moved into places vacated by an Establishment put to flight by the new breed of satirists spawned by *Beyond the Fringe* and *Private Eye*.

In the 1970s Britain seems to have suffered a prolonged hangover after the excesses of the previous decade. Ulster, inflation and union troubles were not made up for by entry into the EEC, North Sea Oil, Women's Lib or, indeed, Punk Rock. Mrs Thatcher applied the corrective in the 1980s, as the country moved more and more from its old manufacturing base over to providing services, consulting, advertising, and

Children collecting aluminium to help the war effort, London, 1940s. (*IWM*)

A street party to celebrate the Queen's Coronation, June 1953. (*Hulton Getty Picture Collection*)

expertise in the 'invisible' market of high finance or in IT.

The post-1945 townscape has seen changes to match those in the worlds of work, entertainment and politics. In 1952 the Clean Air Act served notice on smogs and pea-souper fogs, smuts and blackened buildings, forcing people to stop burning coal and go over to smokeless sources of heat and energy. In the same decade some of the best urban building took place in the 'new towns' like Basildon, Crawley, Stevenage and Harlow. Elsewhere open warfare was declared on slums and what was labelled inadequate, cramped, back-to-back, two-up, two-down, housing. The new 'machine for living in' was a flat in a high-rise block. The architects and planners who promoted these were in league with the traffic engineers, determined to keep the motor car moving whatever the price in multi-storey car parks, meters, traffic wardens and ring roads. The old pollutant, coal smoke, was replaced by petrol and diesel exhaust, and traffic noise.

Fast food was no longer only a pork pie in a pub or fish-and-chips. There were Indian curry houses, Chinese take-aways and American-style ham-burgers, while the drinker could get away from beer in a wine bar. Under the impact of television the big Gaumonts and Odeons closed or were rebuilt as multi-screen cinemas, while the palais de dance gave way to discos and clubs.

Punk rockers demonstrate their anarchic style during the 1970s. (*Barnaby's Picture Library*)

From the late 1960s the introduction of listed buildings and conserv-ation areas, together with the growth of preservation societies, put a brake on 'comprehensive redevelopment'. The end of the century and the start of the Third Millennium see new challenges to the health of towns and the wellbeing of the nine out of ten people who now live urban lives. The fight is on to prevent town centres from dying, as patterns of housing and shopping change, and edge-of-town super-markets exercise the attractions of one-stop shopping. But as banks and department stores close, following the haberdashers, greengrocers, butchers and ironmongers, there are signs of new growth such as farmers' markets, and corner stores acting as pick-up points where customers collect shopping ordered on-line from web sites.

Futurologists tell us that we are in stage two of the consumer revolu-tion: a shift from mass consumption to mass customisation driven by a desire to have things that fit us and our particular lifestyle exactly, and

Millennium celebrations over the Thames
at Westminster, New Year's Eve, 1999.
(*Barnaby's Picture Library*)

for better service. This must offer hope for small city-centre shop
premises, as must the continued attraction of physical shopping,
browsing and being part of a crowd: in a word, 'shoppertainment'.
Another hopeful trend for towns is the growth in the number of young
people postponing marriage and looking to live independently, alone,
where there is a buzz, in 'swinging single cities'. Theirs is a 'flats-and-
cafés' lifestyle, in contrast to the 'family suburbs', and certainly fits in
with government's aim of building 60 per cent of the huge amount of
new housing needed on 'brown' sites, recycled urban land. There looks
to be plenty of life in the British town yet.

Swansea: An Introduction

The twentieth century saw the bustling industrial town of Swansea grow into the second city of Wales: a city with a proud history and an exciting future, a city of literature, a city with ambition and a city with great traditions in industry, maritime trade, music, sport and education. Swansea, a town founded by the Vikings around the time of the first millennium, has a backbone of copper and a seafaring tradition which kept it alive over the decades. But there have been tears and grief as well as joy for the friendly city which boasted the first passenger railway in the world and which was in the front line of the industrial revolution.

For three vicious days in February 1941, the German Luftwaffe pounded Swansea, destroying much of the town centre with high explosive and incendiary bombs which caused a fire storm. In all, 387 people died in the raids, and 412 were injured. Hundreds of people were made homeless and numerous shops and offices were razed to the ground. Worshippers at Mount Pleasant Baptist Church thanked God that their chapel, built in 1825, survived the bombs that destroyed a vast area around it. Windows were blown out of the chapel but the building remained intact and was still being used for the service of God by the time of the second millennium. St Mary's Anglican Church, the roots of which can be traced back more than 1,000 years, was not so lucky. The Bloomfield Church, built to mark the beginning of the twentieth century, was destroyed in the raid. It was rebuilt after the war and is worthy of being a cathedral, although this rank has not been bestowed upon it. Within weeks of the raid, King George VI and Queen Elizabeth visited the town, and on a separate occasion the Prime Minister Winston Churchill, not the most popular politician in Wales before the war, also looked in. Like the Royals, he was cheered through the streets.

The damage done to the town on the nights of 19, 20 and 21 February 1941 was such that it was later said that the Nazis provided the demolition gang that cleared the way for a new Swansea, a modern Swansea, to be rebuilt after the war. It was a high price to pay for progress. The war also came to the seas around Swansea. Many vessels were sunk or damaged by German mines, and some remarkable rescues

were made by the brave volunteers who manned the Mumbles lifeboat –
many of them in their seventies, for the young men were serving in the
armed services. Apart from the blitz, it is the sea that has brought the
most pain to the seaside town, surrounded as it is by some of the most
treacherous waters in the world. The Bristol Channel has the second
highest tides in the world and the sea around Swansea Bay, all too often
whipped by gale force winds, has been the graveyard of scores of vessels
over the centuries. Between 1883 and 1947, a total of eighteen Mumbles
lifeboatmen lost their lives answering SOS calls from ships off the South
Wales coast. Four men died in 1883; six more perished in 1903; eight
men lost their lives in 1947, when they braved a vicious storm in a vain
attempt to save a liberty boat, the SS *Samtampa*, which floundered on the
Sker Rocks at Porthcawl. Thirty-nine members of the *Samtampa*'s crew
also lost their lives. The names of the lifeboatmen who died show what a
close-knit community Mumbles has always been. Perhaps the greatest
tribute of all was paid to William Gammon, Coxswain of the ill-fated
1947 boat, when a new lifeboat was named after him. *The William
Gammon* lifeboat now has pride of place in the Maritime and Industrial
Museum, one of the finest of its kind in Britain.

From the early nineteenth century to 1961 the Mumbles Railway ran
along the coast from the town centre to the headland and its pier. Its
claim to fame is that it was the first passenger railway in the world. Tears
were shed as the historic route was closed in 1961. Fortunately, some
relics from those golden days are preserved in a museum alongside the
Maritime and Industrial Museum.

Evidence of the way that Swansea women manned the home front
during the First World War, working at the Hafod factory, can be seen in
photographs provided by the Swansea Museum, which also supplied some
outstanding photographs marking the visit of King George V and Queen
Mary in the early 1920s.

Swansea folk are proud to be called Swansea Jacks, a named linked to
the men of the town who sailed around Cape Horn. Games of rugby
between Swansea and Llanelli are known as battles of the Jacks versus
the Turks. But the name Swansea Jack was also given to a Retriever dog
whose place in history ranks alongside Greyfriars Bobby, who guarded his
master's grave in Edinburgh. In the 1930s Swansea Jack helped to save
27 people from drowning, an outstanding feat which earned him many
awards from animal organisations. Sadly, he died after someone placed
poison in his patch. There's a memorial to this remarkable dog near
St Helen's Rugby Ground.

In 1969 Swansea was elevated from a town to a city, an honour long
overdue. The ceremony was carried out by Prince Charles, who had been
invested as Prince of Wales three months earlier. It has been a hard
apprenticeship for Swansea, always a worthy rival for Cardiff, which had

been made a city in 1905 and named as Capital of Wales in 1955. The rivalry was not just on the football and rugby fields but also in the realms of local government. By the 1990s, Swansea was bold enough to challenge Cardiff in the bid to become the home of the National Assembly of Wales. Cardiff was chosen but Swansea continued to make its mark in many areas. Cardiff was confident that it would win lottery funding for a new 50-metre swimming pool when it demolished the Empire Pool to make way for the Millennium Stadium. The champagne corks popped in Swansea when it was named as the location for the new international-standard pool.

When the National Museum of Wales shocked Cardiff residents by deciding to scrap its maritime and industrial museum and sell the site for £7.5 million to a commercial developer, Swansea took some of the items and expanded their dockside museum into a treasure house. The museum is only a ten-minute walk from the Dylan Thomas Heritage Centre, where an exhibition dedicated to Swansea's legendary poet has been put on display by Jeff Towns, the owner of Dylan's Book Shop in Paradise Alley, an area surrounded by pubs frequented by the world-acclaimed writer. Fans of Dylan Thomas, who was born in Swansea in 1914 and died in New York in 1953, owe a great deal to the enthusiasm of Towns. Dylan's best-known work was *Under Milk Wood*, which included the lines: 'To begin at the beginning: it is a spring, moonless night in the small town, starless and Bible black.' Thomas spent much of his later life in America, and an article published in 1951 included the comment: 'The land of my fathers. My fathers can have it.' The hours that Thomas spent in the taverns of Swansea no doubt laid the foundation to a drinking habit that led to his early death at the age of 39. He once described an alcoholic as 'a man you don't like who drinks as much as you do'.

Dylan Thomas was born at 5 Cwmdonkin Drive. His father, who hailed from Johnstown, Carmarthen, taught English at Swansea Grammar School, where his famous son was a pupil. For a short while in the 1930s he worked as a reporter at the *South Wales Evening Post* in Swansea, a town which at times he both despised and loved – but never forgot. The Kardomah Café crowd, of which he was king, included fellow poets Vernon Watkins, Charles Fisher and John Pritchard, composer Daniel Jones and artists Mervyn Levy and Alfred James. Other companions in those days were broadcaster and writer Wynford Vaughan-Thomas, who reported from a British bomber during a 1,000-plane air raid on Berlin, and the Rev Leon Atkins, who turned the crypt of St Paul's Church into a sanctuary for homeless people. Less friendly associates included Kingsley Amis, the Swansea University lecturer who wrote the best-selling novel *Lucky Jim* and with whom Thomas had at least one verbal punch-up.

The Dylan Thomas years were the foundation stone of the great literature festivals held in Swansea towards the end of the twentieth century. Such festivals, and the dedication of Jeff Towns, will ensure that Thomas's name will not be forgotten in Swansea.

For me, the other famous name connected with Swansea is Harry Secombe, the former Goon, actor and singer who was knighted for his service to entertainment. Sir Harry, whose greatest fan at one time was said to be Prince Charles, is proud of his links with Swansea where his brother, the Rev Fred Secombe, was Vicar of St Peter's Parish, Crockett. In the 1960s the singer Mary Hopkins, from Pontardawe in the Swansea Valley, was in the charts, but even her success was eclipsed by the actress Catherine Zeta Jones of Mumbles, whose early television success in *The Darling Buds of May* led to a Hollywood career and marriage to an American superstar, Michael Douglas. A Swansea girl to the end, she named their first child Dylan in the summer of 2000. On another plane again was legendary Adelina Patti-Nicolini, who gave her name to the Patti Pavilion. She lived at Craig-y-Nos Castle and entertained some of the most famous people of her time. The castle was so popular that a railway station was built there to cater for the guests.

It was on St David's Day in 1987 that Swansea became a cathedral city. It was the day that the Roman Catholic Church in Wales was restructured and the ancient diocese of Menevia was transferred from Wrexham to Swansea, with a Welsh speaking Irishman, the Rt Rev Daniel Mullins, as bishop. St Joseph's Church in Greenhill was elevated to the rank of a cathedral. Greenhill was the Little Ireland area of Swansea, a magnet for countless refugees from the Great Irish Famine of the 1840s.

Swansea rugby stars are too numerous to mention. The All Whites have a record which can match any in Wales and further afield. Among the host of internationals and British Lions produced by the club are Clive Williams, Trevor Evans, Clem Thomas, David Richards, Dewi Bebb, Mervyn Davies and John Faull. Swansea City Football Club was the toast of Britain when the former Liverpool and Wales star John Toshack became manager and took the team from the Fourth to the First Division in successive seasons. Among Swansea-born soccer players from over the years the names of four Welsh international greats come to mind: John Charles, acclaimed the greatest centre-forward of his era, though he was just as good at centre-half; his brother Mel, who played for a number of clubs, including Arsenal; the golden boy Ivor Allchurch; and Cliff Jones, a flying winger for Spurs. Back in the 1950s, the Town team in the Second Division was packed with outstanding talent, and it was only the need to sell its stars that prevented it from going to the top years before Toshack's men.

Swansea may not be the Capital of Wales, but there is no doubt that it is a capital city with a glorious past and a promising future – a place rebuilt from the ashes of the blitz into a city to compare with any in Europe.

Dawn of
a Century

Fairground, 1902. (*City & County of Swansea Museum Collection*)

Schoolboys gather round one of the last trains to run on Mumbles Railway. (*Western Mail and Echo*)

Trippers to Mumbles, 1902. (*City & County of Swansea Museum Collection*)

Mumbles Pier in Edwardian days. (*Western Mail and Echo*)

Crew of the Mumbles lifeboat, *c.* 1903. (*Mumbles Lifeboat History – Carl Smith*)

Passengers aboard the steamer *Brighton*, 1902. (*City & County of Swansea Museum Collection*)

Fishermen at Mumbles in 1902. (*City & County of Swansea Museum Collection*)

The Mumbles lifeboat loading boat returns to the beach in 1907. (*Mumbles Lifeboat History – Carl Smith*)

ALBERT HALL, SWANSEA.

Programme

OF A

GRAND MORNING CONCERT

ARRANGED BY

MADAME ADELINA

PATTI-NICOLINI

Assisted by the following Eminent Artistes (who kindly give their valuable services):

permission of Messrs. Stedle Bros., Photographers, Swansea).

MISS MARIANNE EISSLER,
(SOLO VIOLIN),

MISS CLARA EISSLER,
(SOLO HARP),

MADAME HANNAH JONES,

MR. DURWARD LELY,   MR. NORMAN SALMOND,

SIGNOR BONETTI,   SIGNOR A. ROMILI,
(SOLO PIANOFORTE,)

CONDUCTOR - - - - Mr. WILHELM GANZ,

TO BE GIVEN

On THURSDAY, JULY 12th, 1894,

AT 2.30 P.M.,

FOR THE BENEFIT OF THE SWANSEA HOSPITAL AND POOR OF THE NEIGHBOURHOOD OF CRAIG-Y-NOS CASTLE.

Madame Adelina Patti was the hostess with the mostest at Craig-y-Nos Castle, Swansea, in late Victorian and Edwardian years. This is a poster from a late Victorian show. Madame Adelina founded the Patti Pavilion in Swansea. She died in 1919. (*Western Mail and Echo*)

The Anglican Church in Wales was still part of the Established Church of England when the foundation stone was laid for the new St Mary's Church towards the end of the nineteenth century. (*West Glamorgan Archive Service*)

St Mary's Anglican Church, which opened at the beginning of the twentieth century. (*West Glamorgan Archive Service*)

The Home Front

The Prince of Wales on a visit to Swansea, 1919. (*Chapman, Swansea*)

The first aeroplane to land at Swansea, in 1912. All over the country, the arrival of these new-fangled machines drew huge crowds. (*Western Mail and Echo*)

The opening of the Drill Hall, Swansea, 1912. (*City & County of Swansea Museum Collection*)

Two scenes from the Coronation of George V in 1912: the mayor leaves the town hall (above),
and a children's choir entertains the crowds at the cricket field (below). (*Western Mail and Echo*)

Women making shells. (*City & County of Swansea Museum Collection*)

Women working in the Hafod factory. (*City & County of Swansea Museum Collection*)

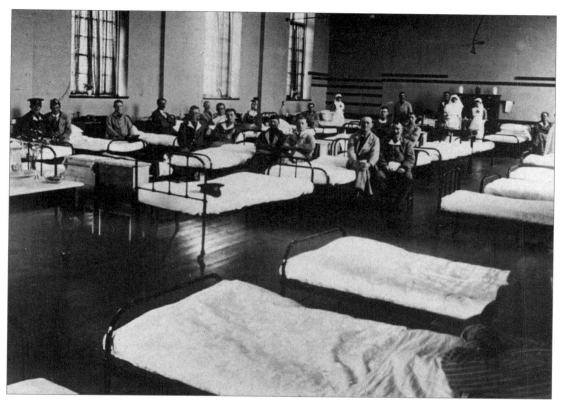

Wounded troops in the Swansea YMCA, which was used as a military hospital in 1918. (*City & County of Swansea Museum Collection*)

The Prince of Wales, who abdicated before being crowned King Edward VIII, in Swansea in 1919. (*Chapman, Swansea*)

Between the Wars

Swansea Jack's memorial. (*Western Mail and Echo*)

King George V on a visit to Hafod Works in the early 1920s. (*City & County of Swansea Museum Collection*)

Queen Mary listens to the choir at Hafod Works. (*City & County of Swansea Museum Collection*)

Hafod workers line up to greet the King and Queen. (*City & County of Swansea Museum Collection*)

A tennis party at Cwmdonkin Terrace, Swansea. (*City & County of Swansea Museum Collection*)

Swansea Jack, the retriever that saved twenty-seven lives. (*Marie Stickler Davies*).

Swansea Jack with some of his friends. (*Marie Stickler Davies*)

Jack's coffin in the living room. (*Marie Stickler Davies*)

The Swansea Jack memorial, put up close to the water front to commemorate a hero remembered by devotees both human and canine. (*Western Mail and Echo*)

Demonstrators in Wind Street in 1920, at the beginning of a wretched decade for working people. The cause espoused by this particular group is not known but transport enthusiasts will appreciate the picture of the electric trolley car. (*Western Mail and Echo*)

War Once More

The stained glass window put in St Mary's Church as a memorial to the victims of the Swansea Blitz. (*Dragon Publishing Ltd*)

The Luftwaffe carried guide maps with them when they came to bomb Wales during the Second World War. Above is a German pilot's view of the Clydach Nicol works and below, the John North Factory. (*Author's collection*)

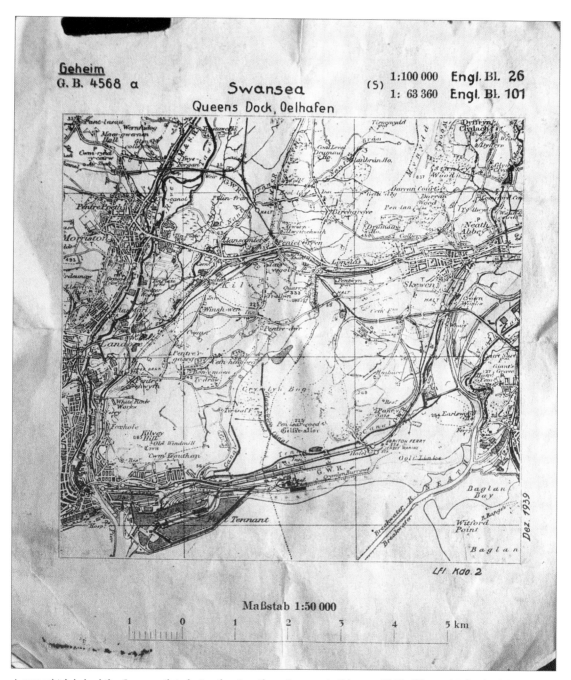

A map which helped the German pilots during the air raids on Swansea in February 1941. (*Western Mail and Echo*)

German bombs destroyed the Kingsway area of Swansea, but by a miracle the Mount Pleasant Baptist Church, established in 1825, survived the carnage. The church suffered broken windows and some minor structural damage but can be seen standing at the rear of the picture. It is still going strong in the new millennium. (*Mount Pleasant Chapel Archives*)

The bombs ripped out the heart of Swansea. Above, the ruins of St Mary's Church can be seen in the background and below, a closer look at the burnt-out shell of the church. (*Western Mail and Echo and City & County of Swansea Museum Collection*)

Christian soldiers battle on: a service held in the ruins of St Mary's Church. (*City & County of Swansea Museum Collection*)

Oxford Street, one of the focal points of the Blitz. (*Western Mail and Echo*)

Men salvaging furniture from among the rubble. (*Western Mail and Echo*)

A Swansea street which the wartime censors would not allow the photographer to name. 'Damage to property in a Welsh coast town' was the caption. (*Western Mail and Echo*)

Rescue workers come
to the aid of a
trapped householder.
(*Western Mail and
Echo*)

If Swansea Docks
were the Germans'
target, they
succeeded in this
raid in February
1941. (*Western
Mail and Echo*)

Thumbs up: a family who survived
the bombing in September 1940.
(*Western Mail and Echo*)

Bombed-out mothers and children in a refuge centre in Swansea. The situation must have been every family's
nightmare, but this group seems to be bearing up well after the 1941 raids. (*Imperial War Museum*)

King George VI and Queen Elizabeth visited Swansea in March 1941, when they paid tribute to the emergency services who were involved in rescue work during the Blitz. (*Western Mail and Echo*)

Prime Minister Winston Churchill also came on a morale-boosting visit in 1941. Above, he is seen with nurses at Swansea Hospital and below, on a walkabout near by. (*Imperial War Museum*)

Churchill acknowledges the cheers of dockers at Swansea in 1941 and below, his car makes slow progress. Showing scant fear of violence, he drives through town in a locally registered open-topped roadster. (*Imperial War Museum*)

Churchill at the Mansion House. His wife Clementine is the imposing figure in the fur coat. (*Western Mail and Echo*)

Still the crowds cheer him as Churchill makes his way home. (*Imperial War Museum*)

Peril at Sea

Coxswain William Gammon, captain of the Mumbles lifeboat, who died in February 1947 with seven of his gallant crew. (*Western Mail and Echo*)

The SS *Santampa*
broke in half after
being wrecked on Sker
Rocks, off Porthcawl.
Thirty-nine members
of her crew died.
(*Western Mail and Echo*)

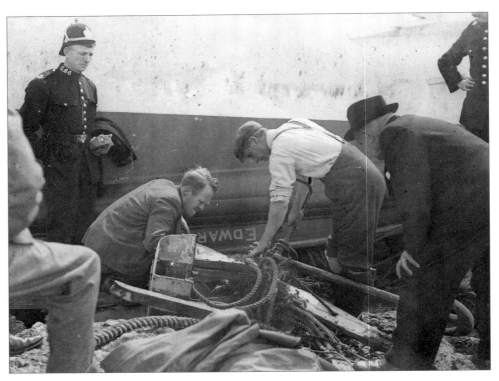

Two RNLI inspectors examine the wrecked lifeboat in which eight of their brave volunteers died. (*Western Mail and Echo*)

Coxswain William Gammon, crewman William Noel and motor mechanic Gilbert Davies. Crewman Richard Smith also perished in the disaster. (*Western Mail and Echo*)

Crewmen R. Thomas and Ernest Griffin. (*Western Mail and Echo*)

Crewman William Howell and his wife Diana, who were married nine years before the disaster. (*Western Mail and Echo*)

Bowman William Thomas, with his wife and children and below, the brave faces of the widows of some of the victims. (*Left: Western Mail and Echo; below: Topical Pictures*)

The heavens wept at the funeral of the lifeboat men in Mumbles on 29 April 1947. (*Press Association*)

Stained glass memorial window at Mumbles
Church. (*Western Mail and Echo*)

The Mayor of Swansea, Alderman Harry Davies,
with the organisers of and subscribers to the
Mumbles Lifeboat Disaster Fund in 1947.
(*Western Mail and Echo*)

Thirty-nine members of the crew of the SS
Samtampa died when the ship was wrecked on
Sker Rocks. The *Samtampa* Memorial is in
Nottage Cemetery, Porthcawl, where relatives of
those who died attended a service of dedication
in April 1949, two years after the tragedy.
(*Western Mail and Echo*)

Tears and Cheers

Playing fields were provided in many parts of Britain in memory of King
George V. This is the Swansea plaque. *(Western Mail and Echo)*

The official opening of King George's Field in 1951. (*Western Mail and Echo*)

King George VI
looks on while
Shirley Dewitt
presents a bouquet
to Queen Elizabeth
in 1951. Shirley's
grandparents were
the Mayor and
Mayoress of
Swansea. (*Western
Mail and Echo*)

Seven people died when
three houses collapsed in
Swansea in September
1950; right, rescuers
search the wreckage of the
properties which did not
survive Hitler's air raids.
(*Western Mail and Echo*)

The body of one of the young victims is taken from the wreckage. (*Western Mail and Echo*)

In a scene chillingly reminiscent of Aberfan a generation later, neighbours watch the rescue operation. (*Western Mail and Echo*)

Children from the Wychtree Street area of Morriston near the spot where a toddler drowned in the Swansea canal. (*Western Mail and Echo*)

Henry Barraclough, chairman of Prince of Wales Dry Dock Company, addresses the crowd at the opening ceremony of the Prince of Wales Dry Dock on 4 June 1959. (*Western Mail and Echo*)

The youngest apprentice, Geoffrey Allen, presents a bouquet of flowers to Mrs Barraclough. (*Western Mail and Echo*)

The Prince of Wales Dry Dock. (*Western Mail and Echo*)

The first passenger on the inaugural flight from Swansea to London in 1959 was Councillor W.T. Mainwaring Hughes, seen with travel agent W.W. Silverson of T.H. Couch. (*Western Mail and Echo*)

The bells for the rebuilt St Mary's parish church arrived from Loughborough in March 1959. (*Western Mail and Echo*)

Swansea Prison, scene of the last executions in Wales. (*Western Mail and Echo*)

Army officers toss coins into the fountain at the former St Paul's church. (*Western Mail and Echo*)

Lord Tedder opens the new BBC studio at Swansea in May 1952. (*Western Mail and Echo*)

Contrasting scenes: above, the view looking east from the Guildhall tower in 1954, with the docks and industrial area in the background and below, the outlook west from the tower, with the beginning of the three-mile green belt which starts with Victoria Park and ends with West Cross. (*Western Mail and Echo*)

Princess Way, the second of Swansea's dual carriageways. This 1952 photograph was taken from the roof of the Midland Bank overlooking the beginning of the new Boots store. (*Western Mail and Echo*)

The birth of a new era. Pupils at St Helen's watch one of the first television sets to be installed in a Swansea school. (*Western Mail and Echo*)

The Honourable Anthony Berry (left), managing director, opened the new Western Mail and Echo Office at Swansea in 1957. He later became a Conservative MP and was killed when an IRA bomb blasted his hotel at Brighton during the party's conference in 1984. (*Western Mail and Echo*)

Crowds at Swansea's new
Fairwood Racecourse in
1959. (*Western Mail and
Echo*)

Punters hoping for a
winner at Fairwood.
(*Western Mail and
Echo*)

Dylan Thomas with his wife Catlin. (*Jeff Towns, Dylan's Book Shop*)

Right: enjoying a game of croquet, a young Dylan Thomas, who grew up to be one of the greatest writers to come out of Wales. (*Jeff Towns, Dylan's Book Shop*)

Right: the famous cigarette shot. Dylan told his Swansea friend Vernon Watkins (above) he thought it made him look tough. Dylan died in 1953. (*Jeff Towns, Dylan's Book Shop*).

End of the Line

A stained glass window tribute to the Mumbles Railway at Oystermouth Parish Church. (*Western Mail and Echo*)

Passengers leave a Mumbles railway car in 1960. (*Western Mail and Echo*)

Nearing the end of the line, on 5 January 1960. (*Western Mail and Echo*)

Passengers disembark after the last scheduled journey on the Mumbles Railway. The final trip was for invited guests only. (*Western Mail and Echo*)

Passengers mourn the loss of the Mumbles Railway. If more people had used it, maybe it would have survived. (*Western Mail and Echo*)

Deputy Mayor Alderman Ken Hare thanks driver Duncan before the last journey on the Mumbles Railway, January 1960. (*Western Mail and Echo*)

Ships wait to put to sea at the Kings Dock lock in 1961. (*Western Mail and Echo*)

Workmen clear the way for the first official car to use the new dual carriageway, mid-1960s. (*Western Mail and Echo*)

Teeing off at the opening of the Swansea Municipal Golf Course, 1960s. (*Western Mail and Echo*)

Students in the refectory of College House, the Students' Union building at Swansea University in 1964. (*Western Mail and Echo*)

Following his Investiture at Caernarfon Castle in July 1969, the Prince of Wales visited Swansea on 15 December of the same year to confer the status of City on the ancient town. He is seen being greeted at the Guildhall by the Mayor, Councillor David Franklyn Bevan. (*Western Mail and Echo*)

Prince Charles delivers his speech at the Guildhall after presenting the City Charter to the Mayor. On the left is the then Home Secretary and future Prime Minister, James Callaghan, MP for Cardiff South-East. (*Western Mail and Echo*)

Prince Charles on a walkabout on the day Swansea became a city. Below, patients in a day room at Singleton Hospital on the same day. (*Western Mail and Echo*)

The Principal of University College Swansea, Professor F. Llewellyn, with Professor Mary Williams outside the new college hall of residence named after her in May 1967. (*Western Mail and Echo*)

Watched by her colleagues, Sister Eleanor Davies feeds a baby in the premature unit at Morriston Hospital in 1967. (*Western Mail and Echo*)

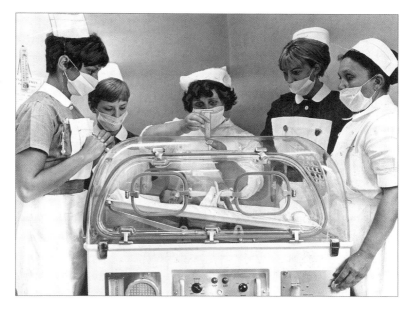

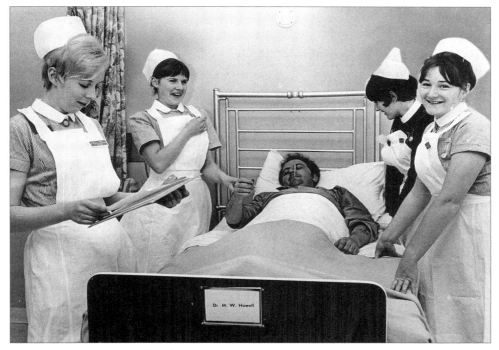

There was plenty of attention for Emlyn Lewis when he was airlifted by RAF helicopter from the Helwick light ship in the Bristol Channel to Singleton Hospital in June 1968. (*Western Mail and Echo*)

Students in the engineering block at Swansea Technical College in 1967. Below, students at the college analyse steel samples in the metallurgy department. (*Western Mail and Echo*)

Great fun at the Swansea Lido in 1964. Right: it looks fun of a different sort in a pottery class at Penlan Comprehensive School in 1962. (*Western Mail and Echo*)

A corner shop in Wern Street, as late as 1964. The white heat of technology did not spread to all areas of Swansea during the Swinging Sixties. (*Western Mail and Echo*)

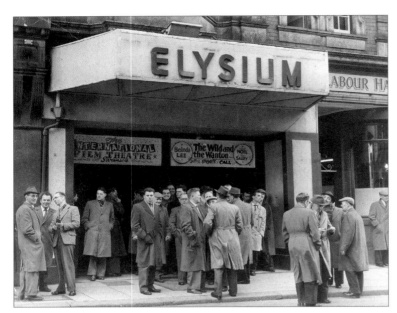

Engineers outside a cinema in the High Street, Swansea, February 1962, take part in a one-day token strike. At this time the Elysium specialised in X-rated shockers. (*Western Mail and Echo*)

Swansea shoppers in the High Street, 1960. (*Western Mail and Echo*)

A busy shopping day just before Christmas in 1960. (*Western Mail and Echo*)

A busy department store on the High Street, 1964. (*Western Mail and Echo*)

The devastated Lower Swansea Valley area, before reclamation took a hold. (*Western Mail and Echo*)

The '60s and into the '70s

A Remembrance Day service at the Swansea Cenotaph, *c.* 1960. (*Western Mail and Echo*)

Leading Swansea City on to the Vetch Field is John Toshack, who managed the club from 1978 to 1983/84 and took it from the Fourth to the First Division in three successive seasons between 1978 and 1981. Below, he is seen with the *Western Mail* team of the year trophy. (*Western Mail and Echo*)

John Toshack with best team trophy. (*Western Mail and Echo*)

A rescue operation was launched in 1970 to save hundreds of fish from the polluted Swansea Canal. (*Western Mail and Echo*)

A scene at Swansea indoor market in 1971. Laverbread was and still is a speciality. (*Western Mail and Echo*)

The Grand Theatre, where many a famous performer has trodden the boards, 1960s. At this time it was more than sixty years old, and was still going strong when it celebrated its centenary in 1995. (*Western Mail and Echo*)

Cathedral City

A memorial window in St Mary's Church to the Welsh troops who lost their lives in the Falklands War in 1982. (*Western Mail and Echo*)

Wooden candlesticks to deter thieves were introduced at St Mary's church in 1983. Canon Dan Lewis, rector, and his wife, the Rev. Ann Lewis, are lighting the candles. (*Western Mail and Echo*)

Henry Owen-John, deputy director of the Glamorgan-Gwent Archaeological Trust, seen in 1988 with a copy of an 1870 print showing where the wall of Swansea Castle was found. (*Western Mail and Echo*)

A restructuring of the Roman Catholic Church in Wales resulted in the Diocese of Menevia being transferred from Wrexham to Swansea on St David's Day 1987. Canon Clyde Johnson is seen reading the Apostolic Mandate. (*Western Mail and Echo*)

Concelebrated Mass at St Joseph's Cathedral, Swansea, when the Menevia Diocese was established there in 1987. Bishop Daniel Mullins was the chief concelebrant. (*Author's collection*)

Altar boys head for the Cathedral. (*Author's collection*)

Priests process to the new Cathedral on 1 March 1987. (*Author's collection*)

Some of the congregation at St Joseph's Cathedral on 1 March 1987. (*Author's collection*)

Bishop Mullins gives communion at the service. (*Author's collection*)

Arriving at Swansea Marina in 1983, the lifeboat *William Gammon*, named after the coxswain of the ill-fated Mumbles lifeboat which was lost with all eight crew members in 1947. The vessel can now be seen at the Maritime and Industrial Museum. (*Western Mail and Echo*)

In 1987 the Mumbles Lifeboat Service was given the Freedom of Swansea. They received the scroll from the Lord Mayor, Councillor Lillian Hopkins. (*Western Mail and Echo*)

Stained glass windows to the memory of Welsh Guards who died in the Falkland War were dedicated at St Mary's Church, Swansea, in December 1985. (*Western Mail and Echo*)

Some of the congregation at Morfa Stadium when the evangelist Dr Luis Palau preached there in May 1989. A multi-million-pound sports stadium is to be built on the site. (*Western Mail and Echo*)

A view of the site of the future Swansea Marina in 1985. (*Western Mail and Echo*)

Swansea University
College Principal Professor
Brian Clarkson with the
President of the Royal
Society of British
Sculptors, Michael
Rizzalio, outside the new
arts centre in 1984.
(*Western Mail and Echo*)

Penclawd cockles are known throughout the world. Seventy-nine-year-old Annie Davies, seen here in 1988 with a basket of cockles, worked on the beach for more than 40 years. (*Western Mail and Echo*)

109

A service to mark the fortieth anniversary of the Mumbles lifeboat disaster of 1947. held in 1987. (*Western Mail and Echo*)

Skylark cruises around Swansea Bay were reintroduced in 1980 for the first time since before the Second World War. (*Western Mail and Echo*)

One of a series of centuries-old clay pits found on the Swansea foreshore in 1982. (*Western Mail and Echo*)

Plans to turn the site of Glanmor School into a public house were strongly opposed by local residents in 1988. (*Western Mail and Echo*)

To mark the fiftieth anniversary of VE Day, Swansea College students Darren James, Parinya Pannoi and Barry Cheng painted this mural at the Royal British Legion Club in Swansea. (*Western Mail and Echo*)

Home Office Minister Ann Widdicombe tastes the porridge at Swansea Prison during an official visit in 1996. (*Western Mail and Echo*)

Hall of Fame

Swansea's famous and favourite son, Harry Secombe, who was knighted for his services to entertainment. (*HTV Wales*)

Swansea-born Goon, comedian and singer Harry Secombe was out-gooned by the choir boys at St Peter's Church, Crocket, Swansea, in 1963. Harry's brother, the Rev Fred Secombe, is in the pulpit. (*Western Mail and Echo*)

A 1984 photograph of Harry Secombe with the Morriston Orpheus Choir at St Thomas Church, Port Tennant, Swansea. (*HTV Wales*)

The All Whites team of 1960. (*Western Mail and Echo*)

Swansea rugby
team celebrate
winning the
SWALEC Cup in
1995. (*Western
Mail and Echo*)

Swansea RFC President W. Roy Jones unveils an honours board commemorating players who had toured with the British Lions including (left to right), Clive Williams, Trevor Evans, Clem Thomas, David Richards, Dewi Bebb, Mervyn Davies and John Faull, 1985. (*Western Mail and Echo*)

Swansea-born Cliff Jones signs for Tottenham Hotspur, watched by Swansea's manager Ron Burgess (standing) and the Spurs' boss Jimmy Anderton, 1958. (*Western Mail and Echo*)

Swansea-born John Charles (right) was one of the greatest soccer players to don a Welsh shirt. He is seen in 1994 receiving an award for his achievements from Brian Mills of Welsh Brewers. (*Western Mail and Echo*)

John's brother Mel was also capped for Wales and had a successful career with Arsenal. (*Western Mail and Echo*)

Swansea's golden boy Ivor Allchurch, hailed as one of the greats of Welsh football. (*Western Mail and Echo*)

117

Singer Mary Hopkins back in her home village of Pontardawe at the height of her fame in 1969. (*Western Mail and Echo*)

The Rt Rev. Rowan Douglas Williams, a native of the Swansea Valley, who was elected Archbishop of Wales in 1999. (*Western Mail and Echo*)

Swansea-born actress Catherine Zeta Jones in her role as Beatrix in *Christopher Columbus, The Discovery*. She became the toast of Hollywood and was planning to marry actor Michael Douglas as this book went to press. (*Rank Films*)

The panels at the Brangwyn Hall in the Guildhall are worthy of a place in any hall of fame. They were originally commissioned from Sir Frank Brangwyn for the House of Lords as a memorial to the dead of the First World War, but the peers found them too brash, so the painter's home town got them instead. Swansea's Director of Music, John Fussell, is seen with one of the panels in 1985. (*Western Mail and Echo*)

Acknowledgements

The author would like to thank the following for their contributions, help and support.

The *Western Mail and Echo* and the generations of photographers who worked for the newspapers; HTV Wales; The Imperial War Museum; Swansea City & County Museum; Swansea Maritime and Industrial Museum; West Glamorgan Archives Department; Dylan Thomas Heritage Centre; Jeff Towns, of Dylan Books; Mumbles Lifeboat Officials; Mumbles Railway Museum; Carl Smith, author of the *History of the Mumbles Lifeboat*; Fr Alun Evans, Rector of St Mary's Anglican Church, Swansea; Governing Body of the Church in Wales; Mount Pleasant Baptist Chapel, Swansea; BBC Wales reporter Gilbert John, R. and S. Brown Printers, Pontardulais; Marie Stickler Davies, author of *Swansea Jack*; Marion Qua.

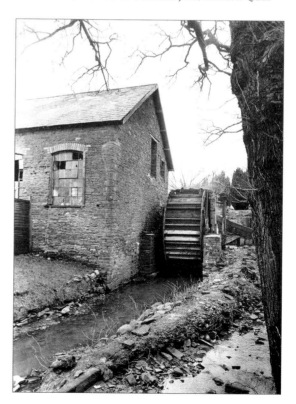

The old corn mill at Cadw, near Gorseinon, was a busy place in Edwardian times. (*Western Mail and Echo*)